EMMANUEL JOSEPH

Nations in the Cloud, Billionaires,
Blockchain, and the Future of Sovereignty

Copyright © 2025 by Emmanuel Joseph

All rights reserved. No part of this publication may be reproduced, stored or transmitted in any form or by any means, electronic, mechanical, photocopying, recording, scanning, or otherwise without written permission from the publisher. It is illegal to copy this book, post it to a website, or distribute it by any other means without permission.

First edition

This book was professionally typeset on Reedsy. Find out more at reedsy.com

Contents

1. Chapter 1: The Digital Revolution and the Dawn of Cloud... — 1
2. Chapter 2: The Billionaire Influence — 3
3. Chapter 3: Understanding Blockchain Technology — 5
4. Chapter 4: Digital Identities and Citizenship — 7
5. Chapter 5: Economic Systems in Cloud Nations — 9
6. Chapter 6: Governance Models in the Cloud — 11
7. Chapter 7: Legal Systems and Dispute Resolution — 13
8. Chapter 8: Education in the Digital Era — 15
9. Chapter 9: Healthcare and Well-being in Cloud Nations — 16
10. Chapter 10: Cultural Identity in the Digital Age — 18
11. Chapter 11: Security and Privacy Concerns — 20
12. Chapter 12: Environmental Impact of Digital Nations — 22
13. Chapter 13: The Role of Artificial Intelligence — 24
14. Chapter 14: The Future of Work in Cloud Nations — 26
15. Chapter 15: Social Dynamics and Community Building — 28
16. Chapter 16: The Global Impact of Cloud Nations — 29
17. Chapter 17: Conclusion and Future Perspectives — 30

1

Chapter 1: The Digital Revolution and the Dawn of Cloud Nations

The digital revolution has ushered in an era of unprecedented technological advancements, transforming how societies function and interact. With the rapid development of cloud computing, blockchain technology, and artificial intelligence, the concept of cloud-based governance has emerged as a potential alternative to traditional nation-states. This chapter explores the rise of cloud nations, their potential impact on traditional sovereignty, and the ethical considerations they present.

At the heart of the digital revolution lies the concept of cloud computing, which allows for the storage and processing of data on remote servers accessible via the internet. This technology has enabled the creation of virtual infrastructures that can support entire communities, economies, and even governance structures. As a result, the idea of nations in the cloud has gained traction, with proponents arguing that cloud-based governance can offer more efficient, transparent, and inclusive systems than their traditional counterparts.

The rise of cloud nations has the potential to significantly alter the concept of sovereignty. Traditional nation-states are defined by their geographical boundaries, centralized governments, and physical infrastructure. In contrast, cloud nations operate in the digital realm, transcending geographical limitations and offering decentralized governance models. This shift challenges the traditional notion of sovereignty, raising questions about the legitimacy, authority, and accountability of cloud-based governance systems.

As cloud nations continue to gain prominence, it is essential to consider the potential benefits and drawbacks of this new form of governance. On one hand, cloud nations can offer more efficient and transparent systems, leveraging technology to streamline processes and reduce bureaucracy. They also have the potential to be more inclusive, providing opportunities for marginalized communities to participate in governance and access essential services. On the other hand, the rise of cloud nations presents ethical concerns, such as the concentration of power in the hands of a few tech moguls, the potential for digital divide, and the risk of eroding traditional cultural identities.

By examining the digital revolution and the dawn of cloud nations, this chapter sets the stage for a deeper exploration of the various aspects of this emerging phenomenon. From the influence of billionaires and the role of blockchain technology to the impact on traditional sovereignty and the ethical considerations at play, the subsequent chapters will delve into the complexities and implications of nations in the cloud.

2

Chapter 2: The Billionaire Influence

The influence of billionaires on society is not a new phenomenon. Throughout history, wealthy individuals have shaped the course of nations, funding wars, shaping policies, and driving economic growth. In the digital era, tech moguls have become the new power players, using their wealth and technological prowess to influence global events and push for transformative change.

Modern-day billionaires, such as Elon Musk, Jeff Bezos, and Mark Zuckerberg, have not only amassed immense wealth but also wield significant influence over technological advancements and societal developments. Their ventures into space exploration, renewable energy, and social media have reshaped industries and created new paradigms. These tech moguls are now exploring the potential of cloud nations, leveraging blockchain technology to create decentralized, digital societies that challenge traditional nation-states.

The influence of billionaires in the realm of cloud nations raises several ethical considerations. While their investments and innovations can drive progress and bring about positive change, the concentration of power in the hands of a few individuals poses risks. The potential for oligarchic control and the prioritization of profit over public interest are critical issues that must be addressed. Ensuring that cloud nations operate with transparency, accountability, and inclusivity is essential to prevent the creation of digital fiefdoms.

In this chapter, we will examine case studies of billionaire-driven initiatives in the digital realm. From Musk's vision of a multi-planetary society to Zuckerberg's ambitions for the Metaverse, these case studies will provide insights into the motivations, challenges, and potential impacts of billionaire-led cloud nations. By understanding the role of these influential figures, we can better navigate the complexities of digital sovereignty.

3

Chapter 3: Understanding Blockchain Technology

Blockchain technology lies at the heart of the concept of cloud nations. As a decentralized, secure, and transparent digital ledger, blockchain has the potential to revolutionize governance, economics, and societal structures. This chapter explores the fundamentals of blockchain technology, its applications in cloud nations, and the benefits and challenges it presents.

At its core, blockchain is a distributed database that allows for secure and transparent recording of transactions. Each block in the chain contains a record of transactions, and once added, these records are immutable. This decentralized nature ensures that no single entity controls the entire system, making it resistant to tampering and fraud.

In the context of cloud nations, blockchain can support decentralized governance structures, enabling transparent decision-making and efficient resource allocation. Smart contracts, self-executing contracts with the terms directly written into code, can automate various processes, reducing bureaucracy and enhancing accountability. Blockchain can also facilitate the creation of digital currencies, providing a secure and efficient medium of exchange within cloud nations.

However, the implementation of blockchain technology in cloud nations is not without challenges. Scalability, energy consumption, and regulatory hurdles are significant concerns that must be addressed. Ensuring that blockchain systems are accessible, secure, and efficient is crucial for the success of digital governance models.

This chapter will delve into the technical aspects of blockchain technology, its potential applications in cloud nations, and the benefits and challenges it presents. By understanding the intricacies of blockchain, we can better appreciate its role in shaping the future of sovereignty.

4

Chapter 4: Digital Identities and Citizenship

As cloud nations emerge, the concept of digital identities and citizenship becomes increasingly important. Digital identities are unique identifiers that individuals use to interact within the digital realm. This chapter explores the process of obtaining digital citizenship, the security and privacy concerns associated with digital identities, and case studies of digital citizenship programs.

Digital identities enable individuals to access services, participate in governance, and engage in economic activities within cloud nations. These identities are typically secured using blockchain technology, ensuring that personal information is protected and transactions are transparent. The process of obtaining digital citizenship often involves verification of identity, similar to traditional nation-states, but with a focus on digital credentials.

While digital identities offer numerous benefits, they also raise significant security and privacy concerns. Ensuring that personal data is protected from cyber threats and unauthorized access is paramount. Blockchain technology can enhance security by providing a tamper-proof record of transactions, but it is not immune to vulnerabilities. Addressing these concerns is essential to building trust in digital identities and citizenship programs.

This chapter will examine case studies of digital citizenship programs, such as Estonia's e-Residency program and various blockchain-based identity initiatives. By exploring these examples, we can gain insights into the challenges and opportunities associated with digital identities and citizenship in cloud nations.

5

Chapter 5: Economic Systems in Cloud Nations

Cloud nations present a unique opportunity to redefine economic systems. This chapter explores the role of digital currencies, blockchain-based economies, and the advantages and challenges of economic models in cloud nations. It also examines case studies of digital economies and their impact on traditional financial systems.

Digital currencies, such as cryptocurrencies, play a central role in the economies of cloud nations. These currencies are built on blockchain technology, providing secure, transparent, and efficient mediums of exchange. Digital currencies enable seamless cross-border transactions, reduce reliance on traditional banking systems, and facilitate financial inclusion.

Blockchain-based economies offer several advantages, including increased transparency, reduced transaction costs, and enhanced security. Smart contracts can automate various economic processes, such as tax collection and welfare distribution, reducing bureaucracy and improving efficiency. However, these digital economies also face challenges, such as regulatory hurdles, scalability issues, and the potential for digital divides.

This chapter will delve into the economic systems of cloud nations, examining the benefits and challenges of digital currencies and blockchain-based economies. By exploring case studies of successful digital economies, we can better understand the potential impact of cloud nations on traditional financial systems.

6

Chapter 6: Governance Models in the Cloud

Cloud nations have the potential to revolutionize governance through decentralized structures and innovative technologies. This chapter explores the various governance models that can be implemented in cloud nations, the role of smart contracts, and the benefits and pitfalls of digital governance.

Decentralized governance structures offer a departure from traditional hierarchical systems, distributing power and decision-making across a network of participants. This approach can enhance transparency, reduce corruption, and promote inclusivity. Blockchain technology enables the implementation of decentralized governance by providing a secure and transparent platform for recording decisions and transactions.

Smart contracts play a crucial role in digital governance, automating processes and ensuring that agreements are executed as intended. These self-executing contracts can streamline administrative tasks, such as voting, resource allocation, and public service delivery, reducing bureaucracy and enhancing efficiency. However, the reliance on code also introduces challenges, such as ensuring that smart contracts are free from bugs and vulnerabilities.

This chapter will examine examples of cloud-based governance models, highlighting their potential benefits and pitfalls. By understanding the intricacies of digital governance, we can better appreciate its potential to reshape the future of sovereignty.

7

Chapter 7: Legal Systems and Dispute Resolution

As cloud nations develop, the establishment of digital legal systems and dispute resolution mechanisms becomes essential. This chapter explores the creation of digital legal frameworks, the role of blockchain in legal systems, and the challenges and opportunities associated with digital dispute resolution.

Digital legal frameworks provide the foundation for cloud-based governance, outlining the rules and regulations that govern digital societies. These frameworks must address issues such as digital identity, data privacy, intellectual property, and cybersecurity. Blockchain technology can support digital legal systems by providing a secure and transparent platform for recording legal transactions and decisions.

Dispute resolution in cloud nations can leverage digital technologies to enhance efficiency and accessibility. Online dispute resolution platforms, powered by smart contracts and blockchain, can automate the resolution of conflicts, reducing the need for traditional courts and legal processes. However, ensuring that digital legal systems are fair, transparent, and accessible to all participants remains a significant challenge.

This chapter will examine examples of digital legal systems and dispute resolution mechanisms, highlighting their potential benefits and challenges.

By understanding the complexities of digital legal frameworks, we can better navigate the legal landscape of cloud nations.

8

Chapter 8: Education in the Digital Era

The digital revolution has transformed the way we approach education, offering new opportunities for learning and skill development. This chapter explores the evolution of digital education, the role of cloud-based education platforms, and the benefits and challenges of digital learning.

Digital education platforms, such as online courses, virtual classrooms, and educational apps, have democratized access to knowledge, allowing individuals to learn at their own pace and from anywhere in the world. Cloud-based education platforms leverage the power of the internet and digital technologies to deliver high-quality educational content, providing opportunities for lifelong learning and skill development.

The benefits of digital education are numerous, including increased accessibility, flexibility, and cost-effectiveness. Digital education can also support personalized learning, allowing individuals to tailor their learning experiences to their unique needs and preferences. However, challenges remain, such as ensuring the quality of digital content, addressing the digital divide, and maintaining student engagement in virtual environments.

This chapter will examine case studies of successful digital education initiatives, highlighting their potential to revolutionize the way we learn. By understanding the evolution of digital education, we can better appreciate its role in shaping the future of cloud nations.

9

Chapter 9: Healthcare and Well-being in Cloud Nations

Cloud nations have the potential to transform healthcare and well-being through digital technologies and innovative solutions. This chapter explores the development of digital healthcare systems, the use of blockchain in healthcare, and the benefits and challenges of digital health initiatives.

Digital healthcare systems leverage the power of technology to deliver high-quality medical services, improve patient outcomes, and enhance the efficiency of healthcare delivery. Telemedicine, electronic health records, and digital health monitoring are just a few examples of how digital technologies are transforming healthcare. Cloud-based healthcare platforms enable the seamless sharing of medical data, facilitating collaboration among healthcare providers and improving patient care.

Blockchain technology can enhance digital healthcare systems by providing secure and transparent platforms for recording medical transactions, protecting patient data, and ensuring the integrity of health records. However, challenges remain, such as addressing data privacy concerns, ensuring the interoperability of digital health systems, and overcoming regulatory barriers.

This chapter will examine examples of digital healthcare programs, highlighting their potential benefits and challenges. By understanding the role of digital technologies in healthcare, we can better appreciate their potential to improve well-being in cloud nations.

10

Chapter 10: Cultural Identity in the Digital Age

The digital age presents both opportunities and challenges for preserving and expressing cultural identity. This chapter explores how cloud nations can help maintain cultural heritage, the role of digital platforms in cultural expression, and the challenges of preserving cultural identity in a digital world.

Digital platforms provide new avenues for cultural expression, allowing individuals and communities to share their traditions, art, and stories with a global audience. Cloud nations can leverage these platforms to celebrate and preserve cultural diversity, fostering a sense of belonging and identity among their digital citizens. Virtual museums, digital archives, and online cultural festivals are just a few examples of how technology can support cultural preservation.

However, the digital age also poses challenges to maintaining cultural identity. The rapid pace of technological change and the influence of global digital culture can erode traditional practices and values. Ensuring that digital platforms respect and honor cultural diversity is essential to prevent the homogenization of cultural identities.

This chapter will examine case studies of digital cultural initiatives, highlighting their potential to preserve and promote cultural heritage. By understanding the role of digital platforms in cultural expression, we can better appreciate their impact on cultural identity in cloud nations.

11

Chapter 11: Security and Privacy Concerns

As cloud nations develop, ensuring the security and privacy of digital citizens becomes paramount. This chapter explores the cybersecurity challenges faced by cloud nations, the role of blockchain in enhancing security, and the privacy concerns associated with digital governance.

Cybersecurity is a critical concern for cloud nations, as digital infrastructures are vulnerable to cyberattacks, data breaches, and other threats. Ensuring the security of digital systems requires robust cybersecurity measures, including encryption, multi-factor authentication, and continuous monitoring. Blockchain technology can enhance security by providing a tamper-proof record of transactions, reducing the risk of fraud and unauthorized access.

Privacy concerns are also a significant challenge in cloud nations. Digital citizens must trust that their personal information is protected and that their privacy rights are respected. Implementing privacy-focused technologies, such as zero-knowledge proofs and decentralized identity systems, can help address these concerns. Ensuring transparency and accountability in data handling practices is essential to building trust in digital governance.

This chapter will examine examples of security measures and privacy-enhancing technologies in cloud nations, highlighting their potential benefits and challenges. By understanding the complexities of cybersecurity and privacy, we can better navigate the digital landscape of cloud nations.

12

Chapter 12: Environmental Impact of Digital Nations

The environmental impact of digital infrastructures is an important consideration for cloud nations. This chapter explores the energy consumption of digital systems, sustainable digital practices, and the potential benefits of digital governance on the environment.

Digital infrastructures, such as data centers and blockchain networks, consume significant amounts of energy, contributing to environmental concerns. Ensuring that these systems are energy-efficient and sustainable is essential to minimizing their environmental impact. Cloud nations can adopt green technologies, such as renewable energy sources and energy-efficient hardware, to reduce their carbon footprint.

Digital governance can also offer environmental benefits by promoting sustainable practices and reducing the need for physical infrastructure. Virtual meetings, digital documentation, and remote work can reduce travel-related emissions and resource consumption. Leveraging technology to monitor and manage environmental resources can also support sustainable development.

This chapter will examine case studies of sustainable digital practices, highlighting their potential to reduce the environmental impact of cloud nations. By understanding the environmental implications of digital infrastructures,

CHAPTER 12: ENVIRONMENTAL IMPACT OF DIGITAL NATIONS

we can better appreciate their role in promoting sustainability.

13

Chapter 13: The Role of Artificial Intelligence

Artificial intelligence (AI) has the potential to revolutionize cloud nations by enhancing governance, decision-making, and service delivery. This chapter explores the integration of AI in cloud nations, the benefits of AI-driven governance, and the challenges and ethical considerations associated with AI.

AI can support cloud nations by automating administrative tasks, analyzing large datasets, and providing personalized services to digital citizens. Machine learning algorithms can identify patterns and trends, enabling informed decision-making and efficient resource allocation. AI-powered chatbots and virtual assistants can enhance citizen engagement and streamline service delivery.

However, the integration of AI in governance also raises ethical considerations and challenges. Ensuring that AI systems are transparent, fair, and unbiased is essential to prevent discrimination and build trust. Addressing the ethical implications of AI, such as privacy concerns and the potential for job displacement, is critical to ensuring that AI benefits all members of society.

This chapter will examine examples of AI-driven governance and explore the ethical considerations associated with AI in cloud nations. By understanding the role of AI in digital governance, we can better appreciate its potential to shape the future of sovereignty.

14

Chapter 14: The Future of Work in Cloud Nations

The digital revolution has transformed the nature of work, creating new opportunities and challenges. This chapter explores the evolution of remote work, the rise of digital nomadism, and the benefits and challenges of digital work environments in cloud nations.

Remote work has become increasingly common, enabled by advances in digital technologies and cloud-based platforms. Cloud nations can leverage these technologies to create flexible and dynamic work environments, allowing individuals to work from anywhere in the world. This shift offers numerous benefits, including increased productivity, improved work-life balance, and reduced commuting-related emissions.

Digital nomadism, the practice of working remotely while traveling, has also gained popularity. Cloud nations can support digital nomads by offering digital citizenship and access to online resources and services. This trend presents opportunities for economic growth and cultural exchange but also raises challenges, such as ensuring access to reliable internet and addressing legal and regulatory issues.

This chapter will examine case studies of digital work initiatives, highlighting their potential to reshape the future of work. By understanding the evolution of remote work and digital nomadism, we can better appreciate their impact on cloud nations.

15

Chapter 15: Social Dynamics and Community Building

The digital age has transformed how we interact and build communities. This chapter explores the dynamics of digital communities, the role of social media in cloud nations, and the benefits and challenges of digital interactions.

Digital communities enable individuals to connect, share experiences, and collaborate across geographical boundaries. Cloud nations can foster these communities by providing platforms for social interaction, collaboration, and civic engagement. Social media plays a crucial role in building digital communities, allowing individuals to express themselves, share ideas, and mobilize for social causes.

However, digital interactions also present challenges, such as the potential for misinformation, cyberbullying, and the erosion of face-to-face communication skills. Ensuring that digital platforms promote healthy and positive interactions is essential to building strong and resilient communities.

This chapter will examine examples of successful digital communities, highlighting their potential to foster social cohesion and civic engagement. By understanding the dynamics of digital interactions, we can better navigate the social landscape of cloud nations.

16

Chapter 16: The Global Impact of Cloud Nations

As cloud nations emerge, their influence on traditional nation-states and global governance becomes increasingly significant. This chapter explores the potential for global collaboration, the challenges of integrating cloud nations into the international system, and case studies of international digital collaborations.

Cloud nations have the potential to foster global collaboration by transcending geographical boundaries and enabling seamless cross-border interactions. This can promote international cooperation, knowledge sharing, and cultural exchange. However, integrating cloud nations into the existing international system presents challenges, such as addressing legal and regulatory issues, ensuring data sovereignty, and navigating geopolitical tensions.

This chapter will examine case studies of international digital collaborations, highlighting their potential to promote global cooperation and address shared challenges. By understanding the global impact of cloud nations, we can better appreciate their role in shaping the future of international relations.

17

Chapter 17: Conclusion and Future Perspectives

The emergence of cloud nations represents a significant shift in the concept of sovereignty and governance. This chapter summarizes the key points discussed throughout the book, explores potential future developments, and considers the ethical considerations and societal impacts of cloud nations.

The rise of cloud nations offers numerous opportunities for innovation, efficiency, and inclusivity. By leveraging digital technologies and decentralized governance models, cloud nations can address many of the challenges faced by traditional nation-states. However, ensuring that these digital societies operate with transparency, accountability, and respect for human rights is essential to their success.

As we look to the future, it is important to consider the ethical implications of cloud nations, such as the concentration of power, data privacy concerns, and the potential for digital divides. By addressing these challenges and promoting inclusive and sustainable digital governance, we can harness the potential of cloud nations to create a more just and equitable world.

This chapter will provide final thoughts on the future of sovereignty and the potential developments in the realm of cloud nations. By reflecting on the key points discussed throughout the book, we can better appreciate the

CHAPTER 17: CONCLUSION AND FUTURE PERSPECTIVES

transformative potential of cloud nations and their impact on the future of governance.

Nations in the Cloud: Billionaires, Blockchain, and the Future of Sovereignty

In a rapidly evolving digital landscape, the concept of nationhood is undergoing a radical transformation. "Nations in the Cloud: Billionaires, Blockchain, and the Future of Sovereignty" explores the emergence of cloud-based governance systems that transcend traditional geographical boundaries and challenge the very notion of sovereignty.

Dive into the revolutionary world of cloud nations, where tech moguls, blockchain technology, and digital identities converge to create new paradigms of governance, economy, and community. From the influence of billionaires like Elon Musk and Mark Zuckerberg to the potential of decentralized governance models powered by blockchain, this book offers a comprehensive and thought-provoking exploration of the future of digital sovereignty.

Discover how digital identities, cloud-based education, and AI-driven governance are reshaping our understanding of citizenship and governance. Uncover the benefits and challenges of digital economies, the environmental impact of digital infrastructures, and the ethical considerations that come with this new era of sovereignty.

With engaging case studies, insightful analyses, and a forward-looking perspective, "Nations in the Cloud" provides a compelling vision of a world where governance is no longer bound by physical borders, but instead thrives in the limitless expanse of the cloud.

www.ingramcontent.com/pod-product-compliance
Lightning Source LLC
LaVergne TN
LVHW020502080526
838202LV00057B/6108